TINY HOTELS

CONTENTS

Florian Siebeck

TINY HOTELS

PRESTEL

Munich · London · New York

DÔMES CHARLEVOIX

3 domes

The small municipality of Petite-Rivière-Saint-François, not far from Quebec City, is the gateway to Le Massif de Charlevoix ski area, a lushly forested mountain region where Canada shows its most Canadian side. In January 2018, a young developer commissioned the Quebec-based architectural firm Bourgeois/Lechasseur to design an eco-resort in the small community that would allow visitors to experience the natural surroundings even more intensely. The result was the Dômes Charlevoix: three geodesic domes that gently nestle against the slope. At night they shine like the eyes of the mountain, but during the day you have to look a little more closely to spot the small igloos. They consist of many little steel triangles (Buckminster Fuller would be proud), covered with a light grey PVC membrane. Although the domes measure barely 50 square metres each, there is enough space for four people in two double beds (one is in a kind of mezzanine, accessible via a small staircase). Nobody has to forego the comforts of a five-star hotel. There is a fully equipped kitchen with dining area, a living room with fireplace, a bathroom with Italian shower – even underfloor heating is installed. The monochrome interior is kept in shades of black and grey. Each dome sits on a wooden deck in which a whirlpool is fitted. From here the view falls over the tops of the maple trees to the Saint Lawrence River. And inside the spheres, the light grey canvas drapes can be pushed aside to reveal a wide panoramic window that offers the same view and allows for stargazing at night. The domes are open all year round thanks to thorough insulation and can withstand even the harshest Canadian winters.

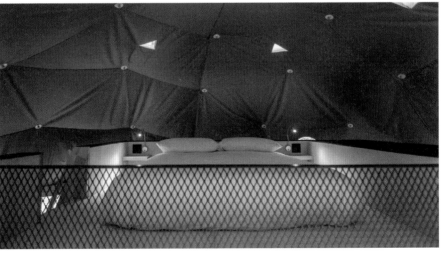

HOTEL COVELL

Los Angeles
United States

9 rooms

Not every dishwasher becomes a millionaire – some also become hoteliers. Dustin Lancaster, for example, did the dishes in a kitchen, became a waiter and then a barman before opening his own bar in Los Angeles at the age of 29. And because there were still five apartments available above, he transformed the house from the 1920s into a tranquil boutique hotel. The Hotel Covell is not divided into rooms but into chapters that tell the life story of the fictional writer George Covell – an idea of the designer Sally Breer, who Lancaster hired to design it. Chapter 1, with its white timber wall panels and uses of dark wood, is a homage to the American Midwest, inspired by George Covell's youth in Oklahoma. Chapter 2 follows him in the 1950s to his New York bachelor pad, with American white oak fittings and furniture by Saarinen and Eames. Chapter 3, with softer colours and textures, is intended to show Covell's bohemian apartment in 1960s Paris, which he shared not only with his beloved Claudine, but also with a pale pink upholstered Bibendum chair by Eileen Gray. And Chapter 4 is a tribute to his voyages around the Old World, a two-bedroom suite somewhere between Morocco and India, with malachite green wallpaper and velvet-covered banquettes. Each of the rooms is accessible via a wood-panelled hallway or an exterior corridor. At first, the story ended with Chapter 5, the apartment of Covell's daughter Isabel, who grew up in Paris and moved to New York in the late 1970s. When Dustin Lancaster recently extended the Hotel Covell to include the neighbouring house, it was immediately clear that the novel would be continued here – in four further chapters following in the footsteps of Isabel Covell.

CALDERA HOUSE

8 suites

Once upon a time there were four friends – three investment bankers and a Pulitzer Prize winner (Wesley Edens, Michael Novogratz, Randal Nardone, and David Barry) – who built themselves a vacation home in the mountains of Wyoming, a pretty impressive one. The Caldera House in Grand Teton National Park (more precisely, in the ski resort of Teton Village, where the favorite means of getting in seems to be the private jet), with its at times retrofuturistic grandeur, is a reminder of the heyday of European ski villages, the Casa del Sole by Italian architect Carlo Mollino and Les Arcs by Charlotte Perriand in Savoy. The spacious chalet, built by local architects Carney Logan Burke, was largely designed by the Californian firm Commune, which also designed the Ace Hotels in Palm Springs and Los Angeles. The Caldera House is more than a boutique hotel; it is an intimate lodge complete with restaurant (the Old Yellowstone Garage serves Italian cuisine), bar, lounge and fitness centre.

The eight spacious suites feel like *pied-à-terres* with floor-to-ceiling windows and mountain views. Four have two bedrooms each spread over 140 square metres, and the others comprise four bedrooms each spread over 470 square metres. Every apartment is finished in a palette of light materials, cedar, white oak and walnut, with the large suites being given a more personal touch. These belong to the owners and are furnished with big-name understatements of modern design – with ottomans by George Nakashima, lamps by Apparatus and a sofa by Vincent Van Duysen. The features also include ultra-modern Boffi kitchens, fireplaces, whirlpools and spacious terraces. The suites are so large that you could almost get lost in them, which would be a pity, because the cable car to the "Roof of the World", as the residents call their summit here, is right outside the front door. How convenient that the concierge of Caldera House is also a ski instructor.

THE INN AT KENMORE HALL

5 rooms

Frank Muytjens and Scott Edward Cole fell in love twice – first with each other, then with a house. The couple had always dreamed of running a small hotel together, as they both enjoy cooking, gardening and entertaining. When Muytjens left his position as head of menswear designer at J. Crew, he gave up his Williamsburg apartment and headed for Massachusetts, where Cole had run a restaurant for a good 20 years. "I passed this house many times in Richmond", says Cole, "but it always remained a mystery to me." Originally built in 1792 for a soldier of the Revolutionary War, Kenmore Hall later housed a prestigious artists' colony where Leonard Bernstein spent his summers. The late-Georgian house in the Federal style, with its symmetrical façade, well-proportioned rooms and spacious corridors – simple yet stately – is surrounded by eight hectares of woods and meadows. The renovation took a mere six months, Kenmore Hall being in remarkably good condition. The colour scheme of the rooms is inspired by Mutyjens's time as a menswear designer: lots of camel, navy, flannel grey and olive, complemented by sensuous elements of wool and leather. Each of the five guest rooms has a fireplace. The interior combines the historic architecture of the house with a unique blend of antiques and mid-century pieces. "Plus books and objects we found on our travels", says Cole. And what was the litmus test for the choice of furniture? Every guest should feel comfortable anywhere in the house with a glass of wine in their hand. The Inn at Kenmore Hall is the ideal starting point for a cultural adventure, as the Tanglewood concert hall and the Massachusetts Museum of Contemporary Art are close by.

THE VILLA CASA CASUARINA

10 suites

It was love at first sight. On his way to a holiday in Cuba, Gianni Versace stopped in Florida in 1992, where his sister Donatella was producing an advertising campaign. And then, on Ocean Drive in Miami Beach, the Italian designer, whose fascination with Greek mythology had turned him into a fashion star for high society, discovered the sculpture of a kneeling Aphrodite. He was so fascinated by the bronze that he wanted to take a closer look, and behind her he found the villa that was to one day become his palace. So the legend goes. The house was built in 1930 in the Mediterranean Revival style by the architect Alden Freeman, modelled after the Alcázar de Colón, the palace built in Santo Domingo between 1510 and 1514 for the son of Christopher Columbus. When Freeman died a little later, the villa became a block of flats. Gianni Versace bought the half-decayed house a few weeks after he had discovered it and radically rebuilt it with eight bedrooms, two kitchens, four living rooms, ten bathrooms, a fitness centre, a steam bath and a shower for eight people. He sent his designers to see his palazzo in Milan, his villa on Lake Como, and through Venice and Versailles; he had furniture upholstered in Versace fabrics, Picassos hung on the walls, and patterns from shawls became the references for trompe l'œils. Instead of pastel colours, Versace opted for gilded wood and dazzling mosaics – the pool is decorated with thousands of small golden Italian tiles. However, his happiness was short-lived. In 1997 Gianni Versace was fatally shot on the steps of his villa. The Villa Casa Casuarina has since then become a boutique hotel that seeks to preserve the eccentric maximalism of this designer of the century in the most faithful manner possible. The splendour of bygone days is more alive today than ever in the ten suites that make up the hotel.

COQUI COQUI COBÁ PAPHOLCHAC

Cobá
Mexico

4 rooms

When the Spanish conquered the Yucatán Peninsula, legend has it that Franciscan monks accompanied them to collect tropical flowers, spices and exotic herbs with the help of the Maya, which they sent back to Queen Isabella of Spain. For almost 300 years – until the Caste War in 1847 – the scents of this "New World" dominated the expansive Spanish Empire. When the Argentinean perfumer Nicolas Malleville heard about this story, he set off for the Yucatán to search after the old aromas on the spot: "I wanted to regenerate original scents, not create something that was intangible or untouchable. My perfumes are simple, naïve, stripped back, so that my children, my grandfather, a Mayan or a Parisian could wear them." Malleville now operates not only a perfumery but also five residences on the peninsula. The most beautiful of these lies in the heart of the dense Yucatán jungle on the banks of a quiet lagoon. With its pyramid-shaped structure, the building echoes the design of the nearby Mayan temples. A stone staircase leads up to two towers, connected by a rope bridge. Two of the four suites are located within these, next to which is a spacious jungle villa. The interior in cream and cocoa tones, with handmade furniture, baths and hammocks, contrasts with the turquoise coloured pools. Old maps, botanical drawings and archaeological photographs recall the golden age of archaeology in the 1920s. Coqui Coqui Cobá Papholchac also houses a perfumery, spa and restaurant. They all work with the fragrances of Nicolas Malleville – including neroli, agave, and tobacco – and turn the hotel into a hideaway in the jungle that appeals to all the senses: a journey through history, scents and tastes.

HOTEL ALAIA

12 suites

When the owner of a narrow coastal strip with the melodious name "El Mirador" wanted to sell his property in 2013, Ramón Navarro's interest was piqued. The professional surfer had grown up nearby in Pichilemu. The town on the Pacific – once a sleepy fishing village – had developed at a rapid pace, becoming a refuge for artists and surfers who rode the waves on the dark sand beaches of Punta de Lobos. A real estate developer published pictures of a gigantic complex of buildings that was to be built there, and Navarro saw only one way to stop him: He would have to buy the land himself. But with what money? "El Mirador" was worth a good million dollars. Through friends, he met the entrepreneur Nicholas Davis and made a deal with him: Davis would advance the money and sell the land to an environmental foundation for a smaller sum. Navarro only had Davis's word, nothing else, but he kept it. The extremely unusual partnership resulted in a nature reserve with a small hotel: Alaia. Chilean architect Nicolas Pfenniger created a design harmonious with the natural landscape, with as little disruption as possible. Demolition wood from an earthquake was used as building material and all 12 suites are fitted with furniture made by local craftsmen. Each bungalow offers direct access to the Pacific Ocean from an outdoor terrace, and of course there is a surf school at which Chile's best surfers teach. A climbing boulder, skatepark and mountain bikes (and yes, also a spa) are provided on land. The hotel's slow food restaurant serves local dishes in harmony with the seasons, including hand-hunted rockfish, freshly gathered shellfish, salt and quinoa from Cáhuil and top wines from the Colchagua Valley. What a tasteful happy ending.

CASA ROBERTO

5 rooms

The Italian journalist Roberto Begnini was sent to Montevideo in 2011 to write about this exciting but rather unknown city. He was so fascinated by the place that shortly thereafter Begnini packed his things and moved there himself. "Montevideo reminds me of the Italy of the 1950s. Despite globalisation, despite the speed of the world, time passes very slowly here." Begnini did not speak a word of Spanish, which did not prevent him from opening his own *maison d'hôtes*: the Casa Roberto. Friends introduced him to an old couple from Florence who wanted to sell their grand town house and move to Paraguay. Built in 1912, the house was commissioned by the English real estate magnate Henry Hamilton and is a prime example of the magnificent architecture of Uruguay at the beginning of the 20th century. "Compared with other old houses, which are usually dark, this one was laid out in an L-shape, making it lighter and brighter." Fortunately for Begnini, the house had been well maintained throughout its hundred-year history. The sumptuous pine floors, the large windows, the central fanlight and the majestic staircase leading to the upper floor had remained practically untouched. Begnini only concerned himself with changing the colour of the walls, decorating them in exciting shades and with English wallpaper. Before its opening in 2016, the interiors journalist scoured the entire city for unique treasures that would complement the building's art nouveau and art deco architecture. He found a cedar console with carved lions' legs for the dining room and a patinated bronze sculpture for the library, which reminded him of a character from Wagner: "I'm still not quite sure whether Wotan or Tannhäuser". Begnini's cabinet of curiosities is "a boutique hotel in the original sense", as he says. All the furniture, chandeliers and works of art can be bought and taken with you.

DÁ LICENÇA

5 suites, 4 rooms

Vitor Borges and Franck Laigneau left their old life in Paris to start a new one in Portugal. Borges had worked as director for textiles and silk at Hermès, and Laigneau was a gallery owner. They were looking for a place to live in Borges's native Alentejo when they came across a number of 19th-century former farm buildings once run by nuns. "For us, it was love at first sight, the gorgeous views, the untouched nature, the magic of the sunsets", says Borges. They decided to share their discovery with guests. Together with the architecture firm Procale, they breathed new life into the houses. The main house now accommodates four guest rooms, while the outbuildings have been converted into five spacious suites (two of which have their own pool; there are two more pools in the common areas). The rooms (50–180 m²), with floors of brushed granite, whitewashed walls and hand-carved baths in pink marble, were furnished by Borges and Laigneau themselves. Laigneau's extensive collection of art and furniture, most of which consists of pieces of Scandinavian art nouveau and from the anthroposophical movement of Rudolf Steiner, is distributed throughout the hotel. "This kind of collection is usually found in museums," Laigneau says, "but we wanted to bring the pieces back to their original context: the home." Both hosts live the ideals of the Arts and Crafts movement: Indeed, they see no difference between furniture and art, which is why the hotel does not feel like a museum or gallery, despite its wealth of artwork. Amidst 120 hectares of olive groves and cork oaks, Vitor Borges and Franck Laigneau now live their new life as hoteliers, making a stay at Dá Licença a feast for the senses. Lunch and dinner are always a surprise; the guests only needs to tell their hosts what they do and do not like.

LE COLLATÉRAL

4 rooms

What have these medieval walls been through? Until the French Revolution, the Sainte-Croix in Arles was a parish church, then a cabaret, then a storehouse for wine and finally a furniture store. And today? Today, the hotel Le Collatéral is located here, in the district La Roquette. It was opened in 2014 by architect and curator Philippe Schiepan and his wife Anne-Laurence. Both have been coming to Arles, the city of the arts, for 25 years and had long wanted to do what many Parisians dream of: start a life in the South. Within 800 square metres they have housed four spacious rooms, a salon and a library. The choice of materials and colours is borrowed from nature. Inspired by the nearby Camargue river delta, the rooms are bathed in ochre, grey, blue and gold – the colours of reeds, water and sand. Artfully crafted mirrors evoke water and its reflection, which is omnipresent here thanks to the nearby Rhône, lakes and the sea. Le Collatéral is also a gallery, although this is not immediately obvious. The specially made furniture and works of art are intended to give the place a depth of meaning, and the majority may also be used. There are regular exhibitions, performances and an artist-in-residence programme, because Le Collatéral is a place of encounters, with history, with art and with guests. The terrace with its view over the roofs of the city is a perfect retreat for free spirits. The owners themselves live in a loft under the roof, and depending on their mood, they also invite guests to their home. "Many clients say they have the impression of living in a piece of art", explains Anne-Laurence Schiepan. It is a living cocoon of art, a hybrid space at the intersection of worlds, in which each guest not only gains a new perspective on life, but also on themselves.

THE HUT B&B

Piercebridge
United Kingdom

2 shepherd's huts

Melanie Phipps had long dreamed of having her own bed and breakfast. Sadly, it would not fit into her two-room London flat. But ultimately, she was lucky that neither she nor her husband Jake – a furniture designer – was tied to the financial metropolis. On the contrary, both wanted to get out of the city and into the fresh air, to the simple life. And so they moved with their children to the north of Yorkshire. Melanie Phipps originally wanted to accommodate their guests in old Airstream caravans, but the aluminium would not have withstood the long and rainy winters in Yorkshire. She discovered shepherd's huts by coincidence, shelters that were used for sheep farming from the 15th into the 20th century, especially in Great Britain and France. The Hut B&B is a small hotel with two carts just behind the house where the family lives with three children, two dogs and nine chickens. One cart is in a field under a large oak tree with a view of the surrounding countryside,

while the other is in the garden between fruit trees and box hedges. "The idea was very simple: I wanted to combine 'glamping' with the benefits of a five-star hotel." Although space is tight at 15 square metres, the proportions were to be generous. The starting point for the design was the bath: "For me, luxury in a hotel means a decent bathroom. I didn't want to settle for less." Instead, Phipps chose to do without a kitchenette – After all, a hearty breakfast is included in the price. Each cart is equipped with a king-size bed, flat-screen TV and Internet. And outside, there are, of course, the people of Yorkshire: "They're friendly, persistent and extremely hard-working – Great people to be around."

LUNDIES HOUSE

7 rooms

With its rugged landscapes, lonely grassy plains, quiet lochs and sleepy corners, hardly any other area of Europe is as sparsely populated as the Scottish Highlands. Here, in the middle of nowhere, Danish fashion entrepreneurs Anders and Anne Holch Povlsen set themselves the task in 2007 of preserving some of the most pristine landscapes in the world. At the same time, they are reviving old country estates. One of their most recent projects is Lundies House on the west coast of Scotland in County Sutherland, a former vicarage from the 17th century that now houses a boutique hotel. The main house has four spacious suites, all with king-size bed and en-suite bathroom, and the small farmstead next door houses studios and a holiday apartment. The Lundies House living room, dining room, kitchen and library are shared by all guests as if it were their own home. Two chefs prepare breakfast and dinner, and in the afternoon, they bake scones and cakes.

The idea of the Povlsens is to make guests feel as if they have landed in the private home of a discerning art collector. This is achieved not only through the paintings and works of art in the house, but above all by the murals of grasses and wild flowers by the French artist Claire Basler. Together with the almost monastically simple interior, which combines Scottish cosiness in the form of velvet and bouclé with understated and minimalistic Scandinavian furniture classics, the Lundies House provides an inviting counterpoint to the harsh landscape on the doorstep. For the design, Anne Holch Povlsen worked together with Ruth Kramer, who runs her own small bed and breakfast, Brücke 49, in the Grisons town of Vals (see p. 98). Kramer even coined a term for this very special style in the Scottish Highlands: "Scandi-Scot."

40 WINKS

2 rooms

David Carter's townhouse in East London has not only welcomed numerous celebrities, it has become a celebrity itself. For more than ten years Carter's cabinet of curiosities has served as a backdrop for *Vogue*, *Tatler* and Burberry, with hundreds of fashion photos being snapped within its walls. When photographers, models and stylists were increasingly asking if it was possible to stay overnight in the 18th-century house, Carter finally decided to transform his home into the 40 Winks Hotel in 2009 ("to take forty winks" means "to take a nap"). There is no sweeping entrance hall and there is no marble in the lobby (how could there be? – there isn't even a lobby), there is no gym, no flatscreens and no whirlpool. "40 Winks offers an escape from the relentless demands of our everyday lives. This is something rare in a city like London", says Carter, who finds that his everyday life has not much changed since the transformation of his house. He simply shares it with guests. And each guest is given a personal welcome into the world of 40 Winks, since David Carter still lives here. He has reserved two rooms for guests on the top floor. The look of 40 Winks – Carter furnished the house himself – is somewhere between a palazzo and a stately home turned opium den, between Alice in Wonderland and Marie Antoinette. *Vogue* once wrote, "A banker goes into this hotel as a banker and leaves as a pervert." The walls of the kitchen are decorated in neoclassical trompe l'œil, the bathroom is covered with golden wallpaper by de Gournay, and somewhere there is a dog on wheels. Every object here tells its own story. The 40 Winks indulges Carter's passion for the playful and the strange; the host is clever, funny and wonderfully quick-witted. He is an old-school dandy who also likes to give advice: "I would like to think that 40 Winks offers guests an experience that does help restore their determination to make the most of life, and to remind them that there is beauty all around us." It is hardly surprising that the waiting list for reservations runs to several months.

SWEETS HOTEL

28 suites spread over the city

Amsterdam's reputation as the "Venice of the North" was established in the 16th century when the city's leaders began to build canals to transport goods from A to B. The shipping traffic was controlled by bridge keepers whose small houses were spread all over town. When control of the bridges was fully automated in 2009, not only were the bridge guards out of a job, but the bridge houses were suddenly empty as well. The architects of Space & Matter then presented the city council with a box containing 28 small models – The idea of a new hotel was born. With the name Sweets Hotel, it became reality. None of the 12 to 70-square-metre houses is like any other. They bear witness to five centuries of Amsterdam's architectural history: from noble classicism to the geometric-ascetic De Stijl movement and the detail-loving brickwork eccentricities of the Amsterdam School, as well as contemporary functional buildings. The oldest cottage is around 350 years old, while the youngest dates from 2009. Each one was fitted – in addition to a toilet – with a shower, which was not always easy, and a large double bed, whose position determined the rest of the room layout. The furnishing of the rooms was adapted to each particular architectural style. The infrastructure of the Sweets Hotel relies on local businesses: "Imagine a park as a hotel lobby, the local bar functioning as a concierge and room service coming from the café around the corner." The doors can be opened via app and breakfast is delivered free of charge. Thanks to the panoramic view of the water, ships and traffic, no hotel can come closer to Amsterdam than here. And for those who find the noise of a busy intersection too loud, earplugs are available.

PURS

11 rooms and suites

He just wanted to fulfil his dream of having his own Italian restaurant. "But then half the street was for sale", says Rolf Doetsch. And because he and his wife love to eat out, they brought haute cuisine to their own doorstep and opened three restaurants in their home town of Andernach (with just under 30,000 inhabitants). During the Roman Empire, the city on the Rhine had been a renowned border crossing. The Doetsch couple now want to restore some of this splendour to Andernach. But because hardly anyone can visit three starred restaurants in one day, they also opened two hotels: the Ochsentor and the Purs. The latter is housed in an almost 350-year-old chancellery, for whose renovation the couple hired the Flemish collector, curator and antiques dealer Axel Vervoordt – a man who usually furnishes the homes of celebrities such as Calvin Klein, Robert De Niro and Kim Kardashian. The Purs is his first hotel. "We simply called and asked him", says Rolf Doetsch, and with success. Using antiques selected by Rolf and Petra Doetsch from Axel Vervoordt in Antwerp, he created a composition spanning centuries, continents and social classes, from the Pyrenean shepherd's table, to the French apothecary cabinet, to the secretaire from the reign of George III. He lets post-war art of the Japanese Gutai group and the Düsseldorf Zero movement meet antique farm cupboards and workbenches; the border between fine art and crafts dissolves. "All the different influences now form a unity that lends the rooms a powerful calm", says Vervoordt. "Everything is real, nothing fake. That's what makes the Purs so unique." And then, of course, there is the fabulous food: Chef Christian Eckhardt cooked up two stars for the hotel in no time.

ROBINS NEST BAUMHAUSHOTEL

Witzenhausen
Germany

5 tree houses, 1 log cabin

It was during a trip to Nepal that Peter Becker discovered that he had lost something by living in the city. He had lived in Berlin for seven years, where he ran a small bar and gallery, but it was time for a new beginning. He left the capital and returned to the countryside where he had grown up. At first, he toyed with the idea of taking over his father's recycling business, but eventually decided against it. When a friend came to visit, they went into the forest, lay down in a clearing of beech trees, at one with the earth, "and that's when I had the idea: I'll build a tree house". Ultimately it became multiple tree houses, and in 2014, Peter Becker founded a tree house hotel that is quite unique in Germany. The five houses are supported by the beech trunks alone and are perched up to eight metres above the ground. Since its opening, the hotel has become a meeting place for people who want to make their late dream of a tree house come true – even if only for one night. They yearn for

deceleration and a greater closeness to nature; there is no Internet. In the Waldbar (i.e., forest bar), the proprietor serves breakfast and regional cuisine, but for traditional home cooking, guests are also welcome in the nearby Berlepsch Castle and its restaurants, in the grounds of which the tree house hotel stands. In the future, a modest village is to be created from ten small and large tree nests, to be connected by bridges. Maybe there will be a small swimming pond; the sauna wagon has already been inaugurated. "Sometimes people ask me if I'm lonely here", says Becker, "But here I've rediscovered my connection to nature after all these years. I'm happy."

BRÜCKE 49 PENSION

4 rooms

Ruth Kramer is actually Swiss, but she has spent half her life in Denmark. When, at the age of 50, the fashion and interior designer began thinking about how she could put a new spin on her life, she and her husband Thomas Schacht moved to an alpine valley in Grisons, to Vals. The small village that became world famous thanks to Peter Zumthor's thermal baths had long been a dream destination for the two. "Ruth and I had always toyed with the idea of living away from Denmark", says Schacht. The plan also suited him, as he had resolved to sell his advertising agency when he turned 50: "And then I was able to leave at only 48." In 2010, the two bought a villa in Vals that was over 100 years old, renovated it with great care and turned it into a guest house. The French-style house was designed in Paris and constructed by a local builder in 1902. It is a peculiar building that combines the architectural characteristics typical of the region with strikingly large, high rooms.

They called it Brücke 49 (in reference to the neighbouring Valser Rhine bridge). It is a second home in the Swiss Alps for style-conscious travellers. Inside, Scandinavian design blends with alpine influences, well-weathered furniture and well-known design classics. Furniture by Danish designers such as Finn Juhl, Arne Jacobsen and Børge Mogensen are harmoniously blended in. Brücke 49 is more a house for friends than a hotel. There are only four rooms, a large sitting room with good books and a kitchen where people cook together. The famous thermal baths are within walking distance. In 2019, Kramer and Schacht expanded their jewel in the Swiss Alps by adding the house next door, which had become too large for the neighbour. This now provides accommodations with two apartments and a loft for longer stays. The motto remains the same: "Come as a guest, leave as a friend."

CENTRAL HOTEL & CAFÉ

1 room

"I think every self-respecting city has to have a central hotel", says Leif Thingtved. Since the war, there had been none in Copenhagen, so the set designer simply opened one: the Central Hotel & Café. With only one room and one bed, the hotel in Copenhagen's Vesterbro district is without doubt one of the smallest in the world, but it is also one of the most beautiful. Thingtved had worked for twelve years as a set designer and prop master, amongst other things for the film *Smilla's Sense of Snow*. Then, together with a friend, he bought the 100-year-old house, in whose attic once lived a cobbler who had his shop on the ground floor. Today it houses a small café, from which a narrow staircase leads up to the room. There was no space for Scandinavian minimalism. Emerald-green wallpaper with bustling branches and dark wood fixtures dictate the look of the space. Some of the furniture is custom-made, others constitute found objects from all over the world, for which Thingtved bid on eBay. Most hotel rooms are not made to linger in, says the designer, no matter how big and expensive they are, because they are far too impersonal. "I think we all remember how, as children, we loved to build caves. This room up here is a bit like a little cave. You don't want to leave, just stay in bed, maybe watch some TV or read a nice book." Breakfast is not served on the ground floor, but in Paris. In fact, it is served at Café Granola, one street corner further on. Whoever shows the key to the Central Hotel is guaranteed to be served as if they were a regular guest. The residents of Copenhagen love Café Granola and the small street Værnedamsvej, in which it is located, because amongst the French restaurants, bistros and bars, it feels just like you are in the first arrondissement. That is why locals enjoy calling their street "Little Paris".

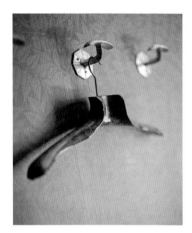

LITLØY FYR

4 rooms

Litløya lies upon the thousand-kilometre-long Norwegian coast, high up in the Arctic. On the "little island", as the name means in English, there are no cars, no shops and above all, no stress. In the 19th century, 75 fishermen still lived here on the outermost edge of the Vesterålen archipelago, while in the cod season there were hundreds. A chapel was built on the island, a school, a prison and in 1912, a lighthouse. The lighthouse is the only one of these buildings still standing today, and only one woman lives on the island: Elena Hansteensen. The Norwegian journalist, who spent many years in Paris, Toronto and the Middle East, always wanted to be close to the sea. In 2006 she bought the lighthouse on Litløya from the coastal administration and promised to open it to the public. She put all her savings into its renovation to open a small hotel, a box seat for the theatre of nature with 360-degree views of the open sea and Lofoten. She has furnished three guest rooms in the former lighthouse keeper's house, with nothing in the neutral coloured rooms to distract from the enormous natural beauty outside, from the rocky islands and cliffs, the wind and the sea and the killer whales that pass by every now and then. The lighthouse accommodates a suite for up to two people. The island can only be reached by boat, and each guest is picked up personally. The trip takes a good 15 minutes. During storms, Litløya is cut off from the outside world. It is a small escape from everyday life, an escape into simplicity. Far away from everything and close only to yourself. The food is as seasonal and regional as it can be. For breakfast, with home-baked bread and scones, there is homemade jam (the berries grow on the island) and herbal tea with fresh mint. For dinner, everyone has to pitch in: harvesting, fishing and setting the table. But soon, Elena Hansteensen also intends to open a small restaurant.

ETT HEM

12 rooms and suites

Hidden behind a small wooden gate in the upmarket district of Lärkstaden – one of Stockholm's best neighbourhoods – is a stylish townhouse made of red brick. It was built at the behest of a high-ranking government official who had not only good taste but also the money to go with it, at the beginning of the 20th century, at a time when people were becoming interested in design and a new aesthetic was born in Stockholm that we know today as Scandinavian modernism. When the current owner Jeanette Mix bought the house to turn it into a hotel, she wanted to preserve the *genius loci* of the place. It was to be "Ett Hem" – "a home". The hotel, therefore, follows a simple philosophy that has often been tried and tested elsewhere but rarely achieved: Every guest should feel as if they were staying with friends. They may turn on the TV, borrow the car, take the dog for a walk or invite friends around. The common rooms on the ground floor (conservatory, kitchen, library and

sitting room) are lined with dark wood, while upstairs twelve bright guest rooms and suites await overnight guests. With its objects, works of art, textiles and furniture, it feels as if the house has been evolving over decades. This is thanks to British designer Ilse Crawford, who worked with sensuous materials such as wicker, wood, marble, leather and velvet. "Luxury is attention, it's care. It's making the ordinary extraordinary", says Crawford. Employees sense when they can have fun with guests, when the guests need something and when they would rather be left alone. As in any good home, life takes place in the kitchen, whose refrigerator is always full. At the communal dining table, you get to know the other guests and eat the home-cooked meals brought to the table. It is almost like being home – Only no one has to clear the plates away.

ONE ROOM HOTEL

1 room

Like a foreign object, Prague's television tower rises out of the city's workers' and artists' quarter Žižkov. Users of a major Internet travel site once voted it the "second ugliest building in the world": a 216-metre-high colossus with steel-clad concrete columns and attached cabins, built between 1985 and 1992. The Žižkov Television Tower is hated by locals, who see it as a symbol of the dark times under communism, a symbol of repression. Its construction, quite literally, called for treading over dead bodies. Parts of the quarter's Jewish cemetery were dug up to pour the foundation. But of all places it is in this building that one of the city's most popular luxury hotels is now located: the One Room Hotel. With its 80-square-metre suite with panoramic view, 68 metres above the ground, the hotel with only one room is almost always booked. The interior is modern. The walls are panelled with light-coloured wood. There is a bed upholstered with horsehair,

two armchairs, a coffee table and a free-standing bath from which guests have the city at their feet. Although guests are by themselves up here, they will find all the usual amenities of a top hotel – from the bar and restaurant to laundry and massage services and even a miniature golf course. A chauffeur with limousine service is available as well as a personal butler who either brings dinner to the room or serves it in the restaurant. The only thing more spectacular is the morning after. The panorama windows offer an unobscured view to the east. The first rays of sunshine fall directly into the room, while the eye wanders over the roofs of Žižkov and the Jewish cemetery to the city limits. By now most Czechs have been reconciled with their television tower, even if some still mock the fact that the greatest luxury of the One Room Hotel is that you do not have to look at the Žižkov Tower when you look out of the window.

VILLA ANTOINETTE

6 rooms

Every summer season the upper crust of 19th-century Viennese society was drawn to the health spa resort of Semmering. Countless colonies of villas were built here, including the Villa Antoinette in 1912. Management consultant Andreas Wessely and interior designer Michael Niederer found the house by chance a few years ago: "We originally wanted to buy a farm and then came across this beautiful but aging guest house." The couple bought the villa with the aim of getting it quickly into shape and ended up working on the renovation for three years. Wessely and Niederer renewed the double casement windows, installed art nouveau tiles from demolished villas, uncovered old doors and had new wainscoting made to order. "We purged the building sins of the 1960s with art nouveau elements", says Wessely. A small rustic snack bar turned into a chalet hotel, Villa Antoinette has six bedrooms, a salon with grand piano, a library and a fully equipped country

kitchen. The adjacent bathhouse boasts floor-to-ceiling panoramic windows, and the spa area includes a sauna, steam bath and outdoor pool. The house has room for 13 guests and is rented as a complete unit; individual rooms are only available upon request. The comfort of a luxury hotel is provided by Mr Edi and Mrs Bibi, the kind souls that look after the house. They take care of everything: guests, luggage and meals. Andreas Wessely and Michael Niederer firmly believe that the health resort of Semmering, with its "architectural jewels, enchanting landscapes and fantastic nature in all seasons" will return to its former glory – not least because of their villa – just as in 1912, when the writer Karl Kraus praised Semmering as an "eternal refuge", as the "place for Viennese society to rendezvous".

CASA POPEEA

11 rooms

The "Pearl of Brăila" in eastern Romania had lost much of its former lustre. The manor house, built in 1900 by a Greek merchant in the art nouveau style, was partially destroyed by fire in 1923. After the Second World War, when it was confiscated by the communist regime, it was increasingly neglected. Ultimately, the collapse of the Soviet Union led to it being left to time and the elements until it was in a state of near collapse. The fact that the listed building now houses a small boutique hotel, the Casa Popeea, is thanks to the architecture offices of Manea Kella and Penta Stil. They restored the house to its original glory, had the building's mighty oak staircase dismantled and sent to a carpentry workshop in Transylvania, while experts on site repaired the moulding and terrazzo floors. The stained oak floors, woodwork and custom-made furniture underscore the restrained, dark colours in the reception area, lobby and café, which open up to a staircase flooded with light. On the upper floor, spacious guest suites were created with minimalist oak furniture, herringbone parquet, brass fixtures and marble. "The new reflects the lost without imitating it", says architect Adrian Manea, who grew up in Brăila and now works in London. The ground floor houses a café and a restaurant, while the architects had the basement converted into a spa dominated by natural materials such as Bulgarian limestone, black marble and stained oak. Casa Popeea is a boutique hotel that effortlessly meets the needs of contemporary travellers without betraying the character of the historic building, to make the "Pearl of Brăila" shine again.

AUTOR ROOMS

4 rooms

Michael Pawlik and his friends from the graphic design practice Mamastudio had a problem: "Whenever friends came to visit, it was almost impossible to find good accommodations for them", says the designer. And so, together with his studio colleagues Magda Ponagajbo and Piotrek Ręczajski, he opened a hotel himself. In one of the few streets of Warsaw largely spared from the destruction of the Second World War, they transformed an old 200-square-metre flat into the Autor Rooms. And what of the fact that none of them had experience in the hotel business? No problem! After all, they had travelled often enough. The hotel, designed by Polish architect Mateusz Baumiller, is divided into four rooms and a central living space. The Autor Rooms is more than a hotel, it is the key to the artistic and creative scene of the entire city. An eclectic mix of custom-made objects by Polish artists, architects, designers and curators blends seamlessly between stucco features and parquet floors. Should an object

appeal to you – even if it is just the door handle – the hosts are happy to put you in touch with its creator. The Autor Rooms fills the gap between cheap hostels, Airbnbs and luxury hotels: "We love our city and know all its secret treasures." The guests meet with locals without having to forego the advantages of a hotel. For example, there is a communal kitchen where guests can cook and chat, but there is also a chef who looks after the guests. In each of the rooms there is a city map including personal tips for Warsaw and a specially produced book featuring the addresses for galleries, artists and craftsmen. In a world dominated by Instagram, the Autor Rooms is not only a treat for the eye, but also a tribute to the creative force of the city. It is not an accommodation, but an adventure.

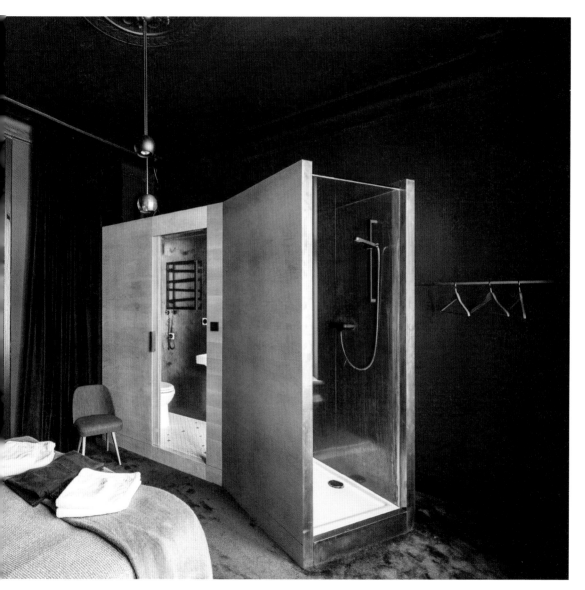

LA PIANTATA

4 rooms, 3 apartments, 2 tree houses

It is a tree house like in an French picture book. But first impressions are deceiving. It is not somewhere in Provence, but in Tuscany. Renzo Stucchi, who had worked for many years as a pastry chef and later as CEO of a fashion company, bought a 40-hectare farm here in 1999, amidst blooming lavender fields and gnarled olive groves – the perfect spot for a bed and breakfast. Nearby there are ancient Etruscan ruins to see and medieval towns and villages along the Via Francigena, the age-old pilgrimage route to Rome. The farmhouse he restored dates from the late 18th century. It is nestled in the wooded landscape around Lake Bolsena, which is considered the cleanest lake in Europe. Stucchi called the property La Piantata: "When I first saw the stately oak tree in the hills, I immediately thought of a tree house", he says. It was not easy to get the planning permission through the Italian bureaucracy, but in 2005 he succeeded, together with French architect Alain

Laurens, who had already built more than 350 wooden houses in trees worldwide. Today, the Suite Bleue is enthroned on the centuries-old oak tree, eight metres above the ground. It can be reached via a spiral staircase and comprises a four-poster bed, bathroom and terrace within a generous 44 square metres. It is not only worth a visit in June and July, when the lavender is in full bloom; the tree house is also open – and heated – in winter. In addition to rooms in his farmhouse, Stucchi also offers a second tree house with an incredible 87 square metres. He has long since turned La Piantata into more than just a bed and breakfast. It is also an organic farm whose product range is revealed at that first meal of the day, with its own pastries, lavender muffins, fresh ricotta, lavender honey and jam, all homemade delicacies which can be brought directly to your bed via pulley – just like in a picture book.

PALAZZO BOZZI CORSO

10 suites

With its baroque palazzi from the 17th century made of volcanic tuff, the Apulian city of Lecce is often called the "Florence of the South". Antonia and Giacomo Fouad Filali, however, have for their part turned the southern Italian city into an Apulian Hollywood. In 2015 the siblings opened their first hotel here, La Fiermontina. They dedicated it to their grandmother Antonia Fiermonte, an artist and muse. This was followed by the Palazzo Bozzi Corso, a five-minute walk away, which pays homage to Antonia Fiermonte's brother, the boxer Enzo Fiermonte, who was married to Lady Astor and starred in more than a hundred films. The Bozzi Corso is housed in a palazzo built in 1775 by the Bozzi noble family from Corsica. It has a typical façade of local limestone with arched balconies and wrought iron railings. Inside its splendour is revealed in a dazzling blend of baroque and modern styles. Lofty pointed vaults and weathered frescoes meet an unconventional colour palette of cream, plum and cobalt blue that, together with furniture classics by Gio Ponti, Carlo Scarpa and Ettore Sottsass, form the backdrop for the owners' tastefully curated art and sculpture collection. It is a calm foretaste of the small museum, which is located outside the walls and tells the story behind the estate and the family: "M.A.M.A." – It is called the Museo Artistico Moderno Antonia, the "Museum of Modern Art Antonia". Each of the hotel suites is dedicated to relatives or friends of the family: René Letourneur and Lady Astor, for example, and John Lennon and Yoko Ono – Anne Filali, the mother of hotel's founder Antonia, is a friend of the artist. The Palazzo almost seems like a mixture of an intimate family home and the Chateau Marmont. Soon the siblings want to export their "La Fiermontina's Collection" to Paris, where they plan to open a branch in the place Vendôme.

TAINARON BLUE

3 rooms

At the southern tip of the Greek mainland, as it has been written for thousands of years, lies the beginning of the end of the world. According to Greek mythology, there is a cave on the Mani Peninsula that serves as the entrance gate to Hades, realm of the god of the underworld. It is stories like these, not to mention the impassable topography, which made this area a refuge for people seeking shelter from persecution right up to the 20th century, and who, once there, had to face the unpredictable Maniot people who were known to fight anyone who got in their way. Even today hundreds of defensive towers along the coast bear witness to these times. During a trip in 1994, Kostas Zouvelos and his wife Kassiani Theodorakakou came across such a tower from the early 19th century that stands 150 metres above the sea and seems to grow out of the rugged mountain landscape. The two architects bought it, initially without knowing what they wanted to do with it, and yet the Tainaron Blue Retreat, which they opened here many years later, seemed like a logical consequence. A four-hour drive south of Athens, Mani is largely untouched despite its excellent hiking trails, historic villages and unspoilt landscape. From the tower one has a spectacular view of the Ionian Sea and the southernmost slope of the Taygetus mountain range. The couple divided the fortified tower into three separate suites and a common dining area, which opens onto a terrace on the roof of a small outbuilding. The interior is of manageable size, but outside (especially in the infinity pool) a sense of boundlessness reigns. In the shade of an olive tree, the chef serves guests traditional dishes such as siglino (marinated smoked pork), the house-style sfougato (spaghetti with mizithra cheese and scrambled eggs) and, of course, freshly baked bread. This is the way to live – but unfortunately only in summer. The retreat is open from May to October.

154

VORA

3 villas

From the infinity pool, which sits on the edge of a rock face that slopes steeply towards the sea, your gaze falls upon the vastness of the Aegean. The villa behind it, with its amorphous vaults, is carved deep into the fissured rock. The Vora is a spectacular hideaway, whose architecture evokes the impressive cave dwellings in which the people of Santorini have lived for centuries, originally out of necessity (wood is practically non-existent on the island) and for protection (to withstand the rigours of the weather). When the island native Yannis Bellonias built the Vora together with the Athenian architectural firm K-Studio, the building was constructed in the same way as a hundred years ago, as little has changed in terms of construction methods. The boutique hotel was carved by hand into the volcanic rock over a period of four years because the terrain is so impassable that it is inaccessible for construction machinery. The Vora consists of a cocoon-like cave villa with three successive rooms that dig deeper and deeper into the rock. There are two newly built villas underneath, each with two floors. The three villas, up to 145 square metres in size, balance between traditional methods of construction and contemporary design. The calming palette of beige and grey tones is contrasted by furniture made from dark brown wood, produced by local artisans. Each villa has a king-size bed, a bath and shower, and a fully equipped kitchen and dining area. A private chef can be on hand if required. Because the villas are set apart from each other, they offer sufficient privacy without guests having to miss a spectacular sunset. This area is called the "Balcony to the Aegean" for a reason.

RIAD MENA

Marrakesh
Morocco

7 suites

There are many riads in Marrakesh, but none like this one. With its tiered terraces, an eight-metre long pool and seven spacious, light-flooded suites, the Riad Mena – seven minutes from the marketplace Jemaa el-Fnaa – is a refreshingly minimalist interpretation of the traditional Moroccan house built around a central courtyard. The owner is Philomena Schurer Merckoll, a German Norwegian who grew up in London. She subsequently lived in Paris, Berlin and New York. When her family bought the 600-square-metre house from the 19th century – originally intended as a private home – she was hooked. Within seven years, Schurer Merckoll restored the riad with the designer Romain Michel-Meniere as carefully as possible to preserve as much of its original character as they could, with its harmonious proportions and carved wood inlays. "I truly believe that every building has its own language and one must always learn to speak this language when restoring something old." In the courtyard garden, together with the Parisian landscape architect Arnaud Casaus, she planted citrus plants, banana trees and palms to accompany the existing orange trees: a green jungle in the Red City. For the riad's restrained colour palette, they used traditional materials such as limestone, tadelakt and cement tiles for walls and floors. The interior lives from a subtle mixture of traditional Moroccan lamps, built-in sofas and modernist furniture by pioneering designers such as Eero Saarinen and Arne Jacobsen, all found at flea markets in Marrakesh. The only thing Philomena Schurer Merckoll brought back from abroad is an extensive library, since "The ultimate luxury is a library with great books – and the time to read them."

GIRAFFE MANOR

12 rooms

Nobody needs a wake-up call here. As early as 6.30 a.m. each morning there is a rustle at the open window as a herd of curious Rothschild's giraffes pass by for breakfast on their way to the national park. The animals slowly trot around the house, sticking their necks in, investigating cheekily whether there is any food about. They manage to stick their long tongues through even the smallest gap – thankfully, room service already makes sure that small glasses of treats are dotted throughout the house. Giraffe Manor was built in 1930, when the first Europeans began to acquire a taste for safaris, but the giraffes have only been around since the seventies. Conservationist Betty Leslie-Melville and her husband Jock bought the ivy-covered manor house from which to raise and later release the endangered Rothschild's giraffes. Although the house is located just outside Nairobi, the wilderness is right around the corner: 57 hectares of forest and bush surround the

manor. In the meantime, Giraffe Manor has become a hotel and spa with 12 rooms in which Kenyan and Old English influences mix. It is hardly surprising that some guests are reminded of *Out of Africa* when they see the stately façade, the elegant interior and the green gardens with sunny terraces: Karen Blixen, the author of the bestselling memoir, happened to live right next door. Some of her furniture can now be found in the rooms of Giraffe Manor. Like the giraffes, hotel guests are permitted to roam the national park during the day, or they can sit on the terrace with a cup of tea. That is where the giraffes tend to drop by again in the late afternoon, often accompanied by some warthogs, before retiring for the night. Who can blame them? They have to get up early.

BISATE LODGE

Volcanoes National Park
Rwanda

6 villas

On the slope of an extinct volcano, nestled in the rolling hills of Rwanda, lies a small boutique resort: Bisate Lodge is the starting point for hikes to visit the last mountain gorillas in the world. Some of these gorillas live in Volcanoes National Park in the north of the country. The six pavilions of the lodge were built into one of the eroded volcanic cones. The unusual architecture of the almost spherical villas, with thatched roofs, ribbed interior walls and floor-to-ceiling windows that offer views of Mount Bisoke, was designed by the South African architectural firm of Nicholas Plewman. The structures are not only reminiscent of the thousands upon thousands of hills that criss-cross this small African country, the design is also rooted in Rwandan building tradition. For example, it borrows from Nyanza's ancient royal palace, which stands as a replica in the former capital of the Kingdom of Rwanda. The villas of Bisate Lodge are no less luxurious: placed around the central

fireplace there is a separate living room and a bedroom with bath. Emerald-green chandeliers made of recycled glass echo the colours of the rainforest, while cowhide rugs and Imigongo art cite the local lifestyle. Imigongo is a Rwandan art form in which geometric patterns are formed from hardened cow dung and then decorated with coloured earth. Since opening, Bisate Lodge has been committed to promoting responsible ecotourism. Activities therefore include not only treks to see the mountain gorillas and golden monkeys, but also excursions to villages (for example, accompanying the chef when he goes to the market to buy ingredients for the day's meals). If you wish, you can also plant a tree; as part of an ambitious reforestation project, the forest has already grown by 15,000 trees.

SHIPWRECK LODGE

10 chalets

Bushmen called the ill-fated coastline in northern Namibia "The Land God Made in Anger" and Portuguese sailors spoke of "The Gates of Hell". Those who were shipwrecked here might have been able to get to land, but the uninhabited and dry coastal desert offered no chance of survival. The wrecks and bones gave this inhospitable spot of earth the name "Skeleton Coast". In 2018, an eco-lodge opened here of all places. The ten chalets, whose abstracted wooden structure is modelled after your emblematic shipwreck, were designed by the architect Nina Maritz. She had read a book by John H. Marsh describing the last days of the MV *Dunedin Star*, a British cargo liner that ran aground on these shores in 1942. The rescue operation by land, sea and air took several months, and only with perseverance could all passengers be saved. "Trying to capture the sense of harshness and desolation that shipwrecked passengers and sailors experienced in earlier times, the timber cabins were designed to evoke broken pieces of ships", says the architect. Nevertheless, there is no need to forego the luxuries of civilisation. Each cabin has electricity and its own bathroom with shower and toilet, and there is even Wi-Fi. A restaurant in the main building serves meals featuring game and fish. From here you can also go on day trips over the bright dunes, past shipwrecks and an abandoned diamond mine to fascinating rock formations and the seal colony in Mowe Bay, where with a little luck you may also see rare brown hyenas. The Skeleton Coast might be hostile and unruly, but it is nature in its most elementary form.

HOTEL MONTEFIORE

12 rooms

The largest concentration of Bauhaus buildings is not somewhere in Germany, but in Tel Aviv. In the 1920s and 1930s, young architects and artists fled Germany in the face of the Nazis, amongst them students of Gropius and Mies van der Rohe. In Tel Aviv they established the International Style. Today, a good 4,000 of these buildings shape the face of the White City. Much less well known is the architectural style that previously dominated the cityscape; in the span of just a few years, hundreds of houses were built in the Eclectic style, almost all of them with bright colours, arches and domes, often similar to each other yet fundamentally different. Many of these buildings have long since been demolished, while others live on, such as the Hotel Montefiore, which is housed in an old Eclecticist residential building dating from 1922. When it opened in 2008, Montefiore was one of the first boutique hotels in Israel – if not the first. It is located in the Lev Halr district, in a small side street off Rothschild Boulevard, one of Tel Aviv's most iconic streets. The lobby is also a restaurant, which with its menu is in some ways the Israeli interpretation of a French-Vietnamese brasserie. Known for its fantastic breakfast and good drinks, people come and go in a constant flow. The 12 rooms of the hotel (8 of them with balcony), which are spread over the two upper floors, offer a haven of peace and quiet. All of them have dark wooden floors and light-coloured walls, stylish furniture and black marble bathrooms. The well-stocked bookshelves reach up to the ceiling, and the walls are hung with works by emerging Israeli artists. With its high ceilings and large windows, the rooms feel light and airy. If you do not think you are in an oasis of peace, just look in the corner – There it is, the palm tree.

MANOUCHEHRI HOUSE

Kashan
Iran

9 rooms

Kashan was never a capital of kings, but that did not take away from its splendour. The merchants who set up stately palaces in the desert here kept countless painters, carpenters, plasterers and glassmakers in the city. With the rise of technology in the 20th century, however, it did not take long for this craftsmanship to disappear, little by little, until the collector Saba Manouchehri bought a nearly dilapidated house in 2008, the origins of which go back to the time of the Safavids. She not only wanted to celebrate the architectural heritage of Kashan by restoring the house, but also its traditions of craftsmanship. The Manouchehri House, which like all houses in Kashan bears the name of its owner, was to become a centre for the textile revival. Kashan had once been a city of fabrics; brocade, velvet and silk were even exported to Europe during the 18th century, and earlier. "Every house had a workshop", she says. But Manouchehri also knows that she must make craft visible in order for it to survive. And so she has opened her house, with its expansive verandas, magnificent honeycomb vaults, mirror works and colourful Orsi windows, to guests. Despite its architectural opulence, interior designer Shahnaz Nader has kept it simple, with minimalist furniture from different eras. "We have also restored the original simplicity of the house with natural materials", says Manouchehri, with wood without lacquer, walls without paint and tiles without glaze. "This creates a feeling of calm." In the garden, accurately pruned fig trees and pomegranate bushes line a long pond. There is a contemporary art gallery, a restaurant and a film room in the house. Manouchehri House was the country's first boutique hotel when it opened in 2011. "When people saw it, they were amazed. And this triggered a movement of restoration in the city", says Saba Manouchehri: "Today, Kashan shines again."

48 LIGHTHOUSE STREET

Galle
Sri Lanka

4 rooms

The city of Galle on the southwest coast of Sri Lanka was once an important seaport for Persians, Arabs, Greeks, Romans, Malays and Indians. In 1663, the Dutch built a fortress here, which is now the largest preserved European fortification in South Asia with a wall that runs to almost three kilometres enclosing the town. Thanks to extensive reconstruction work by Sri Lanka's Department of Archaeology, the historical area is still well preserved. The fortress was declared a UNESCO World Heritage Site because it provides "an outstanding example of an urban ensemble which illustrates the interaction of European architecture and South Asian traditions from the 16th to the 19th centuries." After all, the Portuguese and British were once the colonial masters here. One of the most spacious buildings within the historic ramparts is the boutique hotel 48 Lighthouse Street. The more than 200-year-old manor house has been lavishly restored. Behind the grand doors

hide magnificent interiors with rounded arches and verandas that make you forget the tropical heat and the hustle and bustle around the fort. There are only four rooms, but these are large enough. There is also a living room with ceilings almost eight metres high, a well-stocked library, which houses the owners' book collection and an antique desk, a private bar and a covered terrace. The rooms are furnished with distinguished terrazzo floors, antique doors and windows, and contemporary art hangs everywhere. Three servants, who stay discreetly in the background, take care of the guests' needs around the clock. The historic villa can also be rented in its entirety, but children under 12 years of age are not allowed. For all other guests, 48 Lighthouse Street is a welcome starting point to explore the fortress or to doze in the house's own garden pavilion.

THE SLOW

12 rooms

Tropical brutalism meets relaxed surfer culture in The Slow on Bali. The hotel is owned by fashion designer George Gorrow and his German wife Cisco Tschurtschenthaler, a model he met – as clichéd as it may seem – at a casting call for a fashion show. The Slow is located in Canggu, a village a little north of Seminyak, which attracts plenty of expats with its relaxed surf scene, good restaurants and parties until dawn. Most of them – like Gorrow himself – come from Australia. Originally planned as a private home, The Slow is now one of the best hotels on the island, and since its opening in 2016, it has become a fixed point for surfers and artists. Naked concrete, bamboo furniture, clean lines and bohemian art on the walls not only run through the lobby and restaurant, but also through the twelve rooms, four of which have their own pool on the ground floor. As everywhere in Bali there is a lot of greenery. The house was designed by the Balinese architecture firm GFAB and combines local craftsmanship with urban minimalism. Almost all of the furniture and objects were made especially for the hotel. Instead of the usual amenities with shower caps and sewing kits, the rooms have things that are really needed in Bali: surfboard wax, condoms and body scrub. Instead of televisions, the rooms feature live radio from Los Angeles. Although many top restaurants have been established in Canggu since the hotel opened, The Slow Kitchen & Bar is still a good bet of an evening. At sunset, the hotel's rooftop terrace offers a view of the beach on one side and the mountains on the other, making the problems of life in the big city seem far, far away.

THE BEIGE

11 tents

In 2016, an unusual campsite opened barely twenty minutes from Siem Reap's temple complex of Angkor Wat. The Beige is a Japanese-run resort where guests can escape the world. The eleven stately tents are spread over 2,000 square metres and leave enough space for a secluded stay. A small forest path leads to each tent, all of which are made from organic canvas. Their French-style interiors are reminiscent of times gone by, and every now and then a breeze blows through the open interior, as the tent walls can be opened almost completely to reveal the landscape. The idea of "glamping" is lived out fully at The Beige. Each tent has air conditioning, running water and broadband Internet, an outdoor shower and rocking chairs on the sun terrace. "We want to bring joy to our customers, making them feel a little happier. Hoping it will lead them to have a better life and eventually affect the people around them", say the hoteliers, who provide each guest with a personal contact person and a private driver. The restaurant offers breakfast à la carte and for dinner a menu of traditional Khmer ingredients (such as baby rice and wild honey) and international cuisine; most of the ingredients come from the hotel's own farm. After dinner (or any time you like), The Beige entices with a dip in the forest, not according to the Japanese tradition of *shinrin-yoku* but quite literally. The hotel's large infinity pool is five metres above the forest floor. From its edge you can look out over the treetops to a river in which water buffalos enjoy extensive mud baths, and when the last rays of sunshine touch the treetops, there is hardly any place where you feel more connected to nature than here.

COMO UMA PUNAKHA

9 rooms, 2 villas

Bhutan is the last kingdom in the Himalayas, and Punakha is its granary. The lush valley, which turns into a sea of wild flowers in spring, is dotted with fields and rice terraces where farmers, still wearing traditional clothing, cultivate chillies, aubergines and carrots. Here, on a small hill, the Como hotel group opened a boutique hotel called Uma Punakha in 2012 (the sister hotel is located three hours away at the country's only international airport, in Paro). It is a good starting point, not only for tours to the most beautiful monasteries, temples and villages of the region, but also for trips into almost untouched nature. Around the main house of the resort, which used to belong to a Bhutanese nobleman, there are several buildings boasting a total of nine rooms, and there are also two private villas with butlers. While the architecture is modelled on the country's traditional fortress monasteries, designer Cheong Yew Kuan has kept the interior restrained.

The rooms are furnished with large beds and fireplaces as well as carpets from Nepal. Light enters through floor-to-ceiling windows, and the walls are decorated with traditional murals. The spa is located in a small forest clearing near the resort and offers classic treatments as well as a hot stone bath – a form of traditional Bhutanese medicine. Uma Punakha's restaurant, in turn, is modelled on a traditional fireplace and serves contemporary interpretations of Bhutanese cuisine as well as international dishes. The restaurant is one of the best in the country, with most of the ingredients coming from local farmers. This is a great joy for the resort's up to 20 guests, who can also book the house exclusively for themselves.

TRUNK(HOUSE)

1 house

The Tokyo neighbourhood of Kagurazaka, once the entertainment district of the Edo period, is also called "Little Kyoto" on account of its picturesque alleys. In this area, where Tokyo has retained something of its original spirit, the heart of geisha culture once beat. In an old ryotei, where geishas lived, trained, sang and entertained their male clientele, there is now a boutique hotel that can be booked in its entirety by up to four people: Trunk(House). The exterior has remained true to its history, while the interior combines traditional Japanese aesthetics with contemporary Japanese design over two floors: from its expansive living room with a large brown leather sofa, to the small enclosed garden and the tea room with tatami mats, to a wooden bath of Hinoki cypress in the tiled bathroom, which is unusually large for Tokyo. The bedroom consists of a classic Japanese bed: a mattress resting on a raised wooden platform.

The dining room is characterised by dark walls. It contains a long oak table and a large square windowed door opening onto a small courtyard. Despite all this, Trunk(House) is not a holiday home but a hotel. The difference is not only a private chef, but also round-the-clock service by a team of butlers, who amongst other things are masters of the high art of the tea ceremony. "We wanted to preserve a piece of Kagurazaka's past", says Hiroe Tanaka, Creative Director of Trunk, who designed the hotel in collaboration with Tripster design studio. "Artists and creatives gathered in salons like this one to exchange ideas and thoughts on current affairs, culture and art." And because the new Tokyo should also find its place in Trunk(House), there is a soundproof karaoke bar in bright red, including a disco ball, dance floor and minibar.

PUMPHOUSE POINT

12 rooms on the lake, 7 rooms on land

One of Australia's most spectacular houses is located at the end of a long pier over the country's deepest lake, in the middle of the Tasmanian wilderness. The cream-coloured art deco building on Lake St Clair, about two and a half hours' drive from Hobart, was built in 1940 as a hydroelectric pumping station. The entrepreneur Simon Currant first came across it in the eighties. This temple-like structure in a secluded setting, he thought, would make a perfect hideaway. In fact, apart from a pub five kilometres away, there is nothing to distract from the unspoilt mountain landscape with its extensive myrtle forests and secluded beaches. It took Currant a few years to get permission to carry out his plan, but in the end, he succeeded. In the former pumping station, he opened a twelve-room hotel (there are seven more rooms on land, plus a secluded retreat and restaurant). The interior at Pumphouse Point is purist, with sofas, carpets and blankets in soft shades of grey. Each room is equipped with a small kitchenette and a richly filled pantry. Those who do not wish to cook for themselves can meet for a communal dinner with regional ingredients and Tasmanian wines in the so-called Shorehouse. It would be the perfect holiday for Instagram – if there was Internet. Instead, guests have access to classic board games and a small library in the lounge, whose large windows open onto the majestic mountain lake. During the day, in any case, guests tend to head outdoors, for hiking, climbing and cycling. Or by boat, you can row out onto Lake St Clair, which the Aboriginal Tasmanians reverently call "leeawulenna" – "sleeping water".

ADDRESSES

Brücke 49 Pension 98
Brücke 49
7132 Vals
Switzerland
brucke49.ch

40 Winks 78
Bethnal Green (The full adress will be sent after booking.)
London
United Kingdom
40winks.org

48 Lighthouse Street 192
48 Lighthouse St
Galle 80000
Sri Lanka
elysiumsrilanka.com

Autor Rooms 132
Lwowska 17/7
00-660 Warsaw
Poland
autorrooms.pl

Bisate Lodge 174
Volcanoes National Park
Kinigi, Ruhengeri
Rwanda
wilderness-safaris.com/ bisate-lodge

Caldera House 14
3275 Village Dr.
Teton Village, WY 83025
United States
calderahouse.com

Casa Popeea 128
Strada C.A. Rosetti 1
Brăila 810022
Romania
casapopeea.com

Casa Roberto 50
Maldonado 1159
11100 Montevideo
Uruguay
casaroberto.uy

Central Hotel & Café 104
Tullinsgade 1
1618 Copenhagen
Denmark
centralhotelogcafe.dk

Como Uma Punakha 206
Botokha Kabesa Punakha
Punakha
Bhutan
comohotels.com

Coqui Coqui Cobá Papholchac 38
Lado Sur Laguna Cobá
s/n Solidaridad Q.Roo
87780 Cobá
Mexico
coquicoqui.com

Dá Licença 56
Outeiro das Freiras –
Santo Estêvão
7100-580 Estremoz
Portugal
dalicenca.pt

Dômes Charlevoix 4
54 Chemin Gabrielle Roy
Petite-Rivière-Saint-François
QC G0A 2L0
Canada
domescharlevoix.com

Ett Hem 114
Sköldungagatan 2
114 27 Stockholm
Sweden
etthem.se

Giraffe Manor 168
Gogo Falls Road
Nairobi
Kenya
thesafaricollection.com/ giraffe-manor

Hotel Alaia 44
Camino Punta de Lobos 681
Pichilemu
Chile
hotelalaia.com

Hotel Covell 10
4626 Hollywood Blvd
Los Angeles, CA 90027
United States
hotelcovell.com

Hotel Montefiore 184
Montefiore St 36
Tel Aviv-Yafo 65201
Israel
hotelmontefiore.co.il

Purs 88
Steinweg 30–32
56626 Andernach
Germany
purs.com

La Piantata 138
Strada Provinciale 113
Arlenese
01010 Arlena di Castro VT
Italy
lapiantata.it

Le Collatéral 62

20 Place Joseph Patrat
13200 Arles
France
lecollateral.com

Litløy Fyr 108

Litløya
8470 Bø i Vesterålen
Norway
littleislandlighthouse.com

Lundies House 72

Tongue
Lairg IV27 4XF
Scotland
United Kingdom
lundies.scot

Manouchehri House 188

No. 49, 7th Emarat Alley
Sabet Alley/Mohtasham
Street/
Kashan
Iran
manouchehrihouse.com

One Room Hotel 120

Mahlerovy sady 2699/1
130 00 Prague 3-Žižkov
Czech Republic
oneroomhotel.cz

Palazzo Bozzi Corso 144

Via Umberto I, 38
73100 Lecce LE
Italy
palazzobozzicorso.com

Pumphouse Point 216

1 Lake St Clair Rd
Lake St Clair
TAS 7140
Australia
pumphousepoint.com.au

Riad Mena 160

70 Derb J'Did
Douar Graoua
Marrakesh 40000
Morocco
riadmenaandbeyond.com

Robins Nest Baumhaushotel 94

Berlepsch 1
37218 Witzenhausen
Germany
robins-nest.de

Shipwreck Lodge 178

Skeleton Coast Park
Mowe Bay
Namibia
shipwrecklodge.com.na

Sweets Hotel 84

(The 28 rooms are spread
over the city.)
Amsterdam
The Netherlands
sweetshotel.amsterdam

Tainaron Blue 150

GPS: 36.436773, 22.465654
Oitylo 230 62
Greece
tainaron-blue.com

The Beige 202

GPS: 13.30146, 103.4939
Preak Ko Tmey Village, Svay
Chek Cominue
Angkor Thom District
Krong Siem Reap 17604
Cambodia
the-beige.com

The Hut B&B 68

Holmes House, Piercebridge
Darlington, North Yorkshire,
DL2 3SY
United Kingdom
thehutbandb.co.uk

The Inn at Kenmore Hall 22

1385 State Rd
Richmond, MA 01254
United States
theinnatkenmorehall.com

The Slow 196

Pantai Batu Bolong St No.97
Canggu, North Kuta, Badung
Regency
Bali 80361
Indonesia
theslow.id

The Villa Casa Casuarina 30

1116 Ocean Dr.
Miami Beach
FL 33139
United States
vmmiamibeach.com

Trunk(House) 210

3 Chome-1-34 Kagurazaka
Shinjuku City
Tokyo 162-0825
Japan
trunk-house.com

Villa Antoinette 122

Gläserstraße 9
2680 Semmering
Austria
villa-antoinette.at

Vora 156

Imerovigli 847 00
Santorini
Greece
voravillas.com

Photo Credits

Cover: Shipwreck Lodge, see pp. 178–183. Photo: Shawn van Eeden

5–9 Maxime Valsan
11–13 Danielle Adams
15–21 Douglas Friedman
23–39 Frank Muytjens
31–37 Ken Hayden
39–43 Maya Vishney
45–49 Courtesy of Design Hotels™
51–55 Gianni Franchellucci
57–61 Francisco Nogueira
63 Victor Picon
64 D R, Alice Haldenwang
65 D R

66 Victor Picon
67 Alice Haldenwang
69–71 Topher McGrillis
73–77 Alex Baxter
79–83 Linnea Hurtig
85–87 Courtesy of Sweets Hotel (85, 87 Mirjam Bleeker)
89 Michael Königshofer
90 Lars May
91–93 Michael Königshofer
95 Faruk Pinjo
96 Ana Santl
97 Faruk Pinjo
99–103 Martin Morrell
105–107 Jon Norstrøm
109 Christoph Bouvier
110 Ingebjørg Kårstad
111 Christoph Bouvier
112 Gabi Reichert
113 Lucas Amaral, Christoph Bouvier

115–119 Magnus Mårding
121 Peter von Reichenberg
123–127 Matthias Kronfuss
129–131 Cosmin Dragomir
133–137 Basia Kuligowska, Przemek Nieciecki/Courtesy of Design Hotels™
139–143 Maurizio Brera
145–146 Patrick Locqueneux
147 Bruna Pizzichini
148–149 Patrick Locqueneux
151–155 George Messaritakis

157–159 Claus Brechenmacher, Ståle Eriksen/Courtesy of Design Hotels™
161–167 Richard Powers @ richardpowersphoto
169–173 Courtesy of The Safari Collection
175–177 Courtesy of Wilderness Safaris
179 Denzel Bezuidenhout
180 Michael Turek
181 Martin Harvey (2), Shawn van Eeden
182 Denzel Bezuidenhout
185–187 Courtesy of Hotel Montefiore
189–191 Hamid Eskandari
193–195: Olivia Bonnal Sansoni

197–201 Tommaso Riva
203–205 Zai Nomura
207–209 Martin Morrell
211–215 Tomooki Kengaku/Courtesy of Trunk
217–221 Adam Gibson

Special thanks to Birgit Schmoltner and Sebastian Best

© Prestel Verlag, Munich · London · New York 2020
A member of Verlagsgruppe Random House GmbH
Neumarkter Strasse 28 · 81673 Munich

Prestel Publishing Ltd.
16–18 Berners Street
London W1T 3LN

Prestel Publishing
900 Broadway, Suite 603
New York, NY 10003

A CIP catalogue record for this book is available from the British Library.

Editorial direction Prestel:
Constanze Holler
Translation from the German:
Noel Zmija-Maurice
Copyediting:
José Enrique Macián
Design:
Sofarobotnik, Augsburg & Munich
Production management:
Andrea Cobré

Separations:
Schnieber Graphik, Munich
Printing and binding:
DZS Grafik, d.o.o., Ljubljana
Typeface: Cera
Paper: 170g Primaset

MIX
Paper from responsible sources
FSC® C106600

Verlagsgruppe Random House FSC® N001967

Printed in Slovenia

ISBN 978-3-7913-8672-0

www.prestel.com